hope rises

*Honest stories to honour our babies in heaven
and bring healing to those left behind*

ELIZABETH CHAPMAN

Elizabeth Chapman

South Australia
elizabethchapmanauthor@gmail.com

© Elizabeth Chapman 2022

ISBN: 978-0-6453636-5-4

All rights reserved. Except for private study, research, criticism or reviews, as permitted under the Copyright Act, no part of this book may be reproduced, stored in a retrieval system, or transmitted in any form or by any means without prior written permission. Enquiries should be made to the author.

All contributed testimonies remain the copyright of the respective author and have been used with permission.

All Scripture quotations, unless otherwise indicated, are taken from the Holy Bible, New International Version®, NIV®. Copyright ©1973, 1978, 1984, 2011 by Biblica, Inc.™

Scripture quotations marked (NLT) are taken from the Holy Bible, New Living Translation, copyright ©1996, 2004, 2015 by Tyndale House Foundation. Used by permission of Tyndale House Publishers, Carol Stream, Illinois 60188. All rights reserved.

Scripture quotations marked TPT are from The Passion Translation®. Copyright © 2017, 2018, 2020 by Passion & Fire Ministries, Inc. Used by permission. All rights reserved. ThePassionTranslation.com.

Scripture taken from the New King James Version®. Copyright © 1982 by Thomas Nelson. Used by permission. All rights reserved.

Scripture quotations taken from the Amplified® Bible (AMP), Copyright © 2015 by The Lockman Foundation. Used by permission. www.lockman.org

It is well by Horatio Gates Spafford & Philip Paul Bliss (1873) is in the public domain.

Cataloguing-in-Publications entry is available from the National Library of Australia http:/catalogue.nla.gov.au

First edition published 2022

Why, my soul, are you downcast?
Why do disturbed within me?
Put your hope in God,
for I will yet praise Him,
my Saviour and my God.

Psalm 43:5

In loving memory of Shiloh Grace,
forever in the dwelling place of God.

hope rises

*Honest stories to honour our babies in heaven
and bring healing to those left behind*

*'Hope itself is like a star –
not to be seen in the sunshine of prosperity,
and only to be discovered in the night of adversity.'*

Charles Spurgeon

contents

acknowledgements 1
foreword 3
'me too' 9
tabernacle road 13
'You are still good' 17
truth > triggers 29
oceans 35
survival 41
it's not your fault 45
eternal promises 51
a sound mind 55
two daughters 61
restoration 65
love & prayers 69
speak it 73
the phoenix 77
sacred space 81
ready? set? no 85
songs in the night 89
soon 95
a fable of hope 101
testimonies 105
   to the bereaved mother 107
   my babies 111
   lost & found 118
   the meteorite 122

embracing everest	132
mother of wilde	136
father of wilde	138
not the end	144
your story	148
honouring	154

acknowledgements

JESUS, THANK YOU FIRST AND FOREMOST for not leaving me alone during this season of intense grief. You have my heart forever.

Daniel, I love you. And I love that we have three beautiful children together, even if we haven't had the chance to meet our two girls... yet.

H – our rainbow – thank you for helping me smile.

To Mum, thank you for looking after me when I couldn't look after myself.

To Jenny, thank you for your understanding, love, and support. And especially for those midnight emails...

To Michelle, Lauren, Chelsea, Gail, Helen, Nicole, Jen, Katie, the "Wellspring sisterhood", Matt, and the pastoral team at Journey Uniting, thank you for just being there, and for your love and prayers. And to Sonia – thank you for holding space for me to finally be fragile.

Thank you to the parents who contributed their stories of hope and to Raechel Joyce, a wonderful upcoming author, for writing the foreword for this book.

Because of you all, my hope is rising.

foreword

PREGNANCY LOSS IS A TOPIC I sadly feel professionally qualified to comment on, for thirteen years I've worked as a hospital social worker. Actually, almost for as long as I have known Elizabeth, I've professionally supported families facing every parent's worst fear.

Elizabeth, oh that just sounds way too formal, doesn't it. Liz and I first met at a church we attended together. I was not at all surprised when Liz told me she was going to be studying writing and now even less surprised that she is pursuing a Master of Divinity – they unquestionably encapsulate her passions. Passions Liz holds firm even as she encounters the devastating loss of her precious, much loved and deeply yearned for daughters, Raiya and Shiloh.

The thing I love most about Liz is her concrete, unwavering understanding that being a Christian woman does not exclude her from the effects of sin on all humanity. Romans 5:12 says the origin of death is sin. Liz shares through *Hope Rises*, in a deeply moving heartfelt way, that death can include even the most innocent of all human beings – the yet to be born.

In the many years I have known Liz, her openness to dispel the fear around 'not talked about enough' subjects, coupled with her willingness to be open and vulnerable, gives assent to sharing her own pregnancy loss experiences in real and raw reflections, shared as a testimony of Liz's hope through these profound trials where her faith reigns.

Not only does Liz draw readers into a better understanding of pregnancy loss, using scripture and poetry, but adds depth through bringing together other parents' experiences. *Hope Rises* conveys hope to all who have, or will experience pregnancy loss, empowering freedom to openly feel pain, permission to cry real tears with opportunity to reduce the isolation. *Hope Rises* normalises and validates the humanity of loss, in the spirit of hope.

Hope Rises brings promise to healing through the love of Jesus, through the commonality of God the Father having lost His own Son. Through God's assurance of an end to suffering and an eternity of togetherness, with both Jesus and your very much alive children.

Hope Rises brings purposeful, hopeful meaning when one could easily remain broken, the book is entirely based around healing found through faith in Jesus. Even with my thirteen years of professional experience there is so much more to be learnt that can only be shared through the eyes of a mother's love. *Hope Rises* is superbly written, bringing into the open the 'not spoken about enough' topic of pregnancy loss.

Hope Rises not only offers hope for parents who have experienced pregnancy loss, the book's reflections break fear barriers for those of us who love bereaved parents. In an unexpected discovery while reading *Hope Rises*, I was able to identify more than I initially anticipated, again realising that grief is grief, some absolutely more disenfranchised than other forms, of which pregnancy loss absolutely is; but in all forms of grief there is a need to feel heard, to feel understood, cared for and hopeful.

Hope Rises offers a unique range of experiences and perspectives in healing, which encapsulate the essence of grief and hope through Jesus. Offering both, the ongoing living of a full life on earth, while simultaneously waiting to be reunited with your precious little ones. *Hope Rises* absolutely gives the reader honest stories which honour babies in heaven and bring healing to those left behind.

- Raechel Joyce, author of *The Fairytale of the Jeweller and his Pearl*

*'Hope means hoping
when things are hopeless,
or it is no virtue at all...
As long as matters are really hopeful,
hope is mere flattery or platitude;
it is only when everything is hopeless
that hope begins to be a strength.'*

GK Chesterton

'me too'

THERE'S AN ALMOST CRUEL EXPECTATION to wait to announce a pregnancy until the 12-week mark. *Just in case.* Just in case things aren't okay. Just in case the baby doesn't survive to the second trimester milestone.

So, what if our worst fears become our reality?

Are we expected to suffer in silence?

I will forever be grateful I had sisters in Christ walking alongside me during my pregnancy in those early weeks. My confidence to share must have come from my perfectly healthy pregnancy barely two years prior. But it was a confidence that came crashing down on the 5 September 2021 – Father's Day – when I started spotting. They say there are seven stages of grief. I'm certain I experienced at least four of them that day. Before, during, after...

As I write this, the trauma lingers as though I've only just woken from a nightmare. My body still aches, though the violent cramping and uncontrollable bleeding have finally stopped.

I was ten weeks pregnant. I had a dating scan at seven weeks, when our baby's heartbeat was strong, flickering on the ultrasound machine. But sometime between 12 August and 5 September, our sweet baby went to be with Jesus. I was then forced to experience the horrific physical repercussions of sin and death and the brokenness of this world. The physical cataclysm reached climactic heights in our bathroom that Sunday night. Though the emotional scars from that fateful day are beginning to heal over, they're still raw to touch.

As soon as it happened, I began to reach out. I could think of nothing worse than seeing someone and having them say, 'How far along are you now?' No, everyone I told of the pregnancy, I would tell what happened. I may not have been ready to talk but I sure could text.

I remember that night not wanting to sleep. I wanted to hold onto the day for as long as I could – the day when I still had my baby. Or at least I thought I did. I was too afraid of what the next day would bring. Emptiness? Brokenness? Loneliness?

Of course, even through my tears, I couldn't help but smile. Every time I saw my precious son – a toddler now and the absolute sweetest child – I would smile. I'd hold him close, and my heart would fill with gratitude.

It still does.

Because I know that even in my loss, I am incredibly blessed. Still, I also know that I can be grateful and grieve at the same time.

I know that some women reading this book may not have a child to make them smile in amongst the heartache and I will never understand that hardship, but my heart, in all sincerity, grieves with you...

But whether you have had one miscarriage or more. Whether you have other children or not. Please, let's not fall into the trap of comparison. Our pain is our pain, it doesn't need comparison to legitimise it.

My heart breaks for any woman who has had to endure the loss of a child at any stage of pregnancy or beyond. Nothing in this book is offered as a means of lessening your loss but rather as a way of saying two simple words that bring me so much comfort in this time of grief – 'Me too'.

I will never forget when the doctor was consoling me and she said, 'There is nothing you could have done differently. This happens to one in three pregnancies. It's just not talked about enough...'

Those words struck me – *this* is not talked about enough. Women *need* to hear the words 'me too'. They need to know they are not alone. Because miscarriage can be one of the loneliest experiences.

Even in my lowest moments, I knew God was – *is* – still good. However, there was a sense of deep loneliness, even though I knew He was there. I knew Jesus too had suffered but I struggled to see how Jesus' time on earth and his suffering could possibly connect with what I was going through. It seemed so far removed and it brought a new dimension to the lie of loneliness threatening to overwhelm me. It wasn't until weeks later that two people on the very same day reminded me of this beautiful yet heart-wrenching fact – God the Father knows what it is to lose a child.

Praise be to the God and Father of our Lord Jesus Christ, the Father of compassion and the God of all comfort, who comforts us in all our troubles, so that we can comfort those in any trouble with the comfort we ourselves receive from God. For just as we share abundantly in the sufferings of Christ, so also our comfort abounds through Christ.

2 Corinthians 1:3-5

tabernacle road

IN THE MIDDLE OF WINTER, we decided to travel to one of the coldest destinations in our state for a weekend getaway. It was my husband's birthday and he had been working six-and-a-half days per week for months. Our family needed a break.

Rain swiftly became our travel companion. Not the pretty drizzly kind when you can still do things. No, it was pelting. Only grey haze for as far as the eye could see. A weekend of room service sounded great in theory, only our toddler wasn't convinced.

Leading up to our trip, I had taken a pregnancy test. It was negative and I had to admit, I was relieved. We didn't have *time* for a baby. And if I had been pregnant, it would be nothing short of a miracle anyway since my husband and I had been so busy. So, with that assurance, I even packed a bottle of wine for our getaway. Little did I know, it would go untouched. For the following morning, during my quiet time, a name leapt off the page and into my heart.

Shiloh – 'the dwelling place of God'.

I had been reading Psalm 78, focusing on verses 15 and 16 which describe the Lord providing water in the wilderness after Moses struck the rock. It was for the *Wellspring Devotional Journal* and this passage had been a long time coming for me.

I hadn't known whether the Lord wanted me to be one of the writers for the devotional, I just knew He put the idea on my heart, and I reached out to fellow writers as the Spirit led. Over time, He pruned our team and brought together seven Christian authors who would meditate on different passages in the Psalms and write inspired reflections. After much prayer and back and forth, it became clear I *was* meant to be one of the writers. So, I came to our getaway prepared for a Word. Bible and journal ready, I waited on what the Lord would tell me. To give the two verses context, I read the whole chapter. But instead of being inspired for the devotional – that would come later – He whispered this name in my spirit.

Shiloh.

In those groggy hours before my husband and son awoke, I knew. *If I'm pregnant, it's a girl, and her name is Shiloh.*

Suddenly, I wanted this child. This daughter of promise. I wanted our family of four. Our precious boy and now, a precious baby girl. I whispered prayers over her. *'Please Jesus, let this be true. Let this be Shiloh.'*

So what if we were busy? This was our daughter.

Our Shiloh.

I kept the promise to myself at first and asked the Lord for a sign. That morning it was still raining when we bought takeaway coffees and took our son for a drive. Somehow, in the grey, I spotted a playground. *We should take him there when the weather clears,* I thought. I looked for a street sign so we could find our way back again...

Tabernacle Road.

Tabernacle. The dwelling place of God.

Once we reached a lookout, our son was asleep, and I felt like I had been given the greenlight from the Lord to share this promise with my husband. I began with the words, 'This might sound crazy, but...'

Even my husband couldn't deny the serendipity of the moment.

That afternoon the rain would briefly clear, and we would all play together on that playground. Then, as we reached the car, the first droplet would fall. By the time we were all settled inside, it was pelting again.

But that wasn't the most miraculous part.

In the early hours of Sunday morning in that hotel bathroom, I would receive what the blogosphere refers to as a BFP.

BIG. FAT. POSITIVE.

Splendour and majesty are before Him;
Strength and joy are in His dwelling place.

1 Chronicles 16:27

'You are still good'

WITHIN THE SPACE OF A FEW WEEKS, I was booked in for appointments, tests, and a growth scan on my birthday of all days. She was only 6 weeks and 6 days, but her heart was flickering bright. Everything seemed perfect. I was tired, sure, but only nauseous when I was hungry, same as when I was pregnant with our son. Again, I followed all the rules. I tried to be careful when picking up our one-year-old son and I napped with him as much as I could. I started showing early, around nine weeks. Apparently with number two that can be quite normal. I was already in maternity pants when, on Father's Day 2021, I began to spot. I was ten weeks and two days.

Strangely, the fact that it was Father's Day was a gift in a way – certainly not for my husband. But the family were all there to entertain our son, so I could quietly slip away unnoticed and go to the Women's Assessment Uni at the local hospital.

I will never forget that day.

I waited for what seemed like forever. I wasn't bleeding enough for what warranted concern, but I knew something wasn't right. So, they did a scan. There was nothing on the screen. The nurse tried with an internal scanner that was soon retracted from me more bloodied than I expected it to be. I asked the inevitable question: 'Could I be having a miscarriage?'

She touched my arm. 'It's possible.'

Tears soaked my face mask.

I was going to be referred to someone with an advanced machine, someone who could search for our baby inside of me with more sophisticated equipment. The doctor left me alone for a few moments to dress and I went to the toilet. I told God that I wasn't even going to look at toilet paper this time, I didn't want to see. Only, I couldn't miss the bright red in the toilet bowl.

I begged Jesus for it not to be true. But then, as I saw my broken self in the mirror, I whispered through gritted teeth, *'You are still good. You are still good... No matter what... Even if... You are still good...'*

After an internal examination the doctors instructed me that I was free to go home but if my bleeding filled a pad an hour to call ahead and come back. As I left the hospital and walked to my car seemingly alone, it started to rain. All I could stammer were the same words over and over again. *'You are still good. You are still good... You are still good...'*

My husband was waiting at my parents' house. Earlier he had told me he wasn't worried because our daughter was a promised child. Now, it seemed we were losing her, promised or not. As we stood around with the family, officially marking the worst Father's Day we had ever known, I felt the first gush of blood leave me. I doubled over. Even with this sudden and dramatic increase, it wasn't enough to warrant going back to the hospital. So my husband took me and our son home and Mum remained on standby.

Within moments of being home, the bleeding became uncontrollable.

I will never look at our bathroom the same way again.

I strictly warned my husband to stay out and I got in the shower. My son slept soundly in our bed surrounded by pillows, while I stood in the shower crying out to Jesus. I begged Him to make what I was seeing go away. For it to wash away down the drain. Shock seized me and I honestly thought the clot on the floor was my baby. I didn't know what to do. I called the hospital. I called Mum. I lined up my next steps. But the blood... It was everywhere. A pad an hour? Try a pad every five minutes.

I saw something that in my shock I assumed was the placenta or something? By the time Mum arrived, I had managed to clog our toilet and put my evidence in a container for the doctors. Then my husband took me to the hospital.

Another internal. Then they analysed what I had brought in. The *something* I had seen was a sac. They called it some sort of medical term.

But it was our baby.

I was utterly broken, depleted, bleeding, and cramping.

There are no words.
Nothing to say.
My pen runs dry,
The parchment tears.
There are no words.
Not one to write.
I search in vain.
There are no words.

Slowly, the bleeding eased so I could at least lay down and rest. But I did *not* want to sleep. Sleep meant waking up *tomorrow*. And tomorrow meant that I wasn't pregnant that day. At least if I held onto today, I was still pregnant that day. Sort of. At least, that was what raced through my mind as I sobbed into my pillow.

*I don't want to sleep
and leave today
when you were still here*

They say we 'lost' you
If only that were the case
For then we might find you
This side of eternity

The next week was a blur of take-away and painkillers. And I finally opened that bottle of wine...

Seven days and I'm still here.
The world moves on and disappears.
The flowers wilt, the thoughts run dry.
Only prayer gets me through the night.
Seven days and I'm still here,
Wishing for the time when you were near.

But God's grace was so vivid during this time, it was almost tangible. Flashbacks haunted me, awake or asleep, and it was in that pain that I was gifted a vision. I began to reimagine it all again, but with Jesus physically *with* me...

He was there. Every moment.
I can see him now.
Forehead to mine.
Squeezing my hand.
Tears in His eyes as I prayed,
'Please, Jesus!'
'I'm sorry it has to be this way...'
Tears, pain, blood. So much blood.
By the time I saw my child,
She was already in His arms.
'You are still good...
You are still good...
You are still good...
You are still good...
You are still good...'

Here my cry, O God;
listen to my prayer.
From the ends of the earth I call to you,
I call as my heart grows faint;
lead me to the rock that is higher than I.

Psalm 61:1-2

truth > triggers

LANDMINES WERE EVERYWHERE.
The first time I went shopping on my own after the miscarriage, I was shocked at how many people had babies. *How had I not noticed before?* I was shocked further when my old faithful stationary store didn't have a decent journal and I had to resort to going to Target and walking straight through the baby department to arrive at stationary. I found a journal to start recording my thoughts, prayers, poetry, and Bible verses, but it came at a cost far higher than the five or so dollars. My insides were an anxious mess. My mind spun as I tried to avert my gaze from the tiny floral singlets.

This should be me. I should be shopping here. I shouldn't be buying a journal to record all these feelings of loss.

They say grief is just love with nowhere to go, but I wanted mine to go somewhere, to do something. To be tangible and real. To live outside of me. Otherwise, there was no telling how far this love would go to find a place to belong.

Long before this season of grief, a fellow mother shared how a friend had been pregnant at the same time as her when she was having her son. Devastatingly, however, her friend miscarried. Even now, years later, her friend still behaved strangely around her son.

I didn't understand it at the time. But I do now.

She was measuring.

So, this is how old my child would be...

Perhaps there was also some envy and thoughts of unfairness.

I don't think I'll be able to help but watch the children grow who are born around Shiloh's due date and wonder what she would be like? Like this friend, I'll measure.

I wonder if she'd be a good sleeper or a cat napper like her brother?

Another birthday? They grow up way too fast.

So, she would be starting school this year...

Maybe one day these triggers will fall to the back of my mind but for now I have no choice but to combat each one of them with truth.

This is not a means of 'getting over' triggers or lessening the pain, it's simply a way of refocussing the mind and not allowing emotions to consume me. There are three simple phrases:

I am not alone

I am not broken

God is still good

I AM NOT ALONE.
Miscarriage and pregnancy loss can feel like the loneliest path. It can feel like everyone is pregnant except for you, that everyone has children except for you. But you are not alone. If this book serves as anything it is a reminder that you are not alone. Not only are there parents pouring their hearts onto these pages, but our Heavenly Father is here, catching our every tear.

You keep track of all my sorrows.
You have collected all my tears in your bottle.
You have recorded each one in your book.

Psalm 56:8 (NLT)

I AM NOT BROKEN.
The world is broken. These tragedies that have occurred in our lives are the result of sin entering the world. Please take that in for a moment, please don't dismiss it as common Christian knowledge. This world is not the way God intended it to be. But even so, you were made in the image of God. You are His beloved daughter. You are not broken. This world is broken, and the enemy wants you to think it's all you. Don't believe the lie. Please. We are redeemed through Jesus Christ and one day He is coming to make all things new.

I praise you because I am fearfully and wonderfully made;
your works are wonderful,
I know that full well.

Psalm 139:14

He who was seated on the throne said, 'I am making everything new!' Then he said, 'Write this down, for these words are trustworthy and true.'

Revelation 21:5

GOD IS STILL GOOD.

The reason I have clung to this phrase is because I know I can't give the enemy a foothold in my life. Even when we don't understand, even when it's beyond any hardship we have ever endured – God is still good. He is a good God. He loves us so completely. Rest on that truth when everything else seems to be spiralling out of control, claim it out loud over and over. On an overcast day, we don't doubt the heat of the sun or its ability to ignite the sky. Likewise, when we are navigating our way through grief and the grey abyss seems overwhelming, we can know that we have a God who is good, who will comfort us and strengthen us.

Submit yourselves, then, to God.
Resist the devil, and he will flee from you.

James 4:7

The Spirit of the Sovereign Lord is on me, because the Lord has anointed me to proclaim good news to the poor. He has sent me to bind up the broken-hearted, to proclaim freedom for the captives and release from darkness for the prisoners, to proclaim the year of the Lord's favour and the day of vengeance of our God, to comfort all who mourn, and provide for those who grieve in Zion—
to bestow on them a crown of beauty instead of ashes, the oil of joy instead of mourning, and a garment of praise instead of a spirit of despair. They will be called oaks of righteousness, a planting of the Lord for the display of his splendour.

Isaiah 61:1-3

oceans

A BLACK OCEAN swarming with powerful waves of anxiety and depression threatened to overwhelm me and swallow me whole. The only thing that kept me from sinking, the one thing that kept me from willingly throwing myself aboard and indulging those waves, and maybe even my selfish heart, the only One who anchored me in the truth of God's goodness and faithfulness was Jesus. This ocean was wild and vicious. Not the shallows by the shore but rather the untamed open waters where every creature unimaginable lingered beneath its immense and seemingly fathomless depths. Our ships may be tossed to and fro, but we have an anchor holding us secure.

We have this certain hope like a strong, unbreakable anchor holding our souls to God himself. Our anchor of hope is fastened to the mercy seat in the heavenly realm beyond the sacred threshold, and where Jesus, our forerunner, has gone in before us. He is now and forever our royal Priest like Melchizedek.

Hebrews 6:19-20

So, what can navigating these foreign oceans of grief even look like? Practically?

For me, it looked a little like this...

~ I immersed myself in God's Word and searched for devotionals specifically on miscarriage.

~ I journaled and prayed. A lot.

~ I reached out to sisters in Christ who I knew would pray fervently for me.

~ I played worship music through my headphones.

~ I emailed my dear friend in the middle of night, almost every night following the miscarriage.

~ I cried. Hard.

~ I was gentle with myself, I let responsibilities around the home slide.

~ I asked for help.

~ I started speaking to a Christian counsellor weekly.

~ I did what I needed to in the moment, I listened to my body.

~ I allowed myself to *feel*. And to tell God about it.

I swiftly learned that God could handle it. Whatever stage of grief we are in, He knows and He understands.

Even in our darkest moments, He doesn't abandon us but speaks to our soul through His Word, which is living and active. The Amplified translation of Hebrews 4:12 states, *'For the word of God is living and active and full of power [making it operative, energising, and effective]. It is sharper than any two-edged sword, penetrating as far as the division of the soul and spirit [the completeness of a person], and of both joints and marrow [the deepest parts of our nature], exposing and judging the very thoughts and intentions of the heart.'*

Living. Active. Powerful.

This is the Word of God Almighty.

The following words might have been penned long before our time but I'm sure we can relate to the depths of darkness and seeming hopelessness of the psalmist in Psalm 88.

Lord, you are the God who saves me;
day and night I cry out to you.
May my prayer come before you;
turn your ear to my cry.

I am overwhelmed with troubles
and my life draws near to death.
I am counted among those who go down to the pit;
I am like one without strength.
I am set apart with the dead,
like the slain who lie in the grave,
whom you remember no more,
who are cut off from your care.

You have put me in the lowest pit,
in the darkest depths.
Your wrath lies heavily on me;
you have overwhelmed me with all your waves.
You have taken from me my closest friends
and have made me repulsive to them.
I am confined and cannot escape;
my eyes are dim with grief.

I call to you, Lord, every day;
I spread out my hands to you.
Do you show your wonders to the dead?
Do their spirits rise up and praise you?
Is your love declared in the grave,
your faithfulness in Destruction?
Are your wonders known in the place of darkness,
or your righteous deeds in the land of oblivion?

> *But I cry to you for help, Lord;*
> *in the morning my prayer comes before you.*
> *Why, Lord, do you reject me*
> *and hide your face from me?*
>
> *From my youth I have suffered and been close to death;*
> *I have borne your terrors and am in despair.*
> *Your wrath has swept over me;*
> *your terrors have destroyed me.*
> *All day long they surround me like a flood;*
> *they have completely engulfed me.*
> *You have taken from me friend and neighbour—*
> *darkness is my closest friend.*

So, even when the storm rages and the darkness feels overwhelming, we have a God who calms oceans.

Then (Jesus) arose and rebuked the wind, and said to the sea, 'Peace, be still!' And the wind ceased and there was a great calm. But He said to them, 'Why are you so fearful? How is it that you have no faith?'

Mark 4:39-40

survival

I DIDN'T WANT TO FORGET OUR BABY, but even in the intense grief, there were brief moments when I began to feel somewhat 'okay', in the vaguest sense of the word. I started wondering about our future, even if it involved me figuratively scrounging around on the floor trying to pick up the strewn pieces of my pre-pregnancy plans. It was in these fleeting moments when the most intense blows of guilt would thump me in the gut, sending me doubled over and stumbling in pain. How could *anything* go back to the way it was? A whole life had been lost. Our baby was in heaven. How could I 'get on' with life after losing my child? How could I stop thinking of what happened for a moment to consider something else? What sort of mother *was* I?

Guilt.
Guilt.
Guilt.
Guilt.
Guilt.

I confessed these feelings to my husband, small silver linings like: *I don't have to give birth again anytime soon... I can keep writing, publishing, and studying... I won't be balancing two kids next year...*

Even saying it 'out loud' made me anxious that I was a terrible mother. But as it turned out, I was just an honest one trying to hold onto anything positive. Because as my husband and I both knew, I would rather have laboured for hours on end, given up my vocations, and done my all for our two children, than to live every single day in this alternate reality.

He gently reminded me that it wasn't awful.

It was *survival*.

Of course, part of me wanted to revert to *basic* survival – to stay completely and utterly miserable to remember our baby. Part of me wanted to stay in that place of barely functioning, barely sleeping, barely being myself, because of guilt.

Sometimes survival is taking a step forward. Just one, even if it's as tiny as your precious one's foot would have been. But a step, nonetheless. And a guilt-free one at that.

My counsellor would later confirm that these positive thoughts – the silver linings, the sparks of light in the darkness of those early stages of grief – is what discerns a person of faith. It is Jesus in them. It is Jesus in *me*.

It is hope rising.

How enriched are they who find their strength in the Lord;
Within their hearts are the highways of holiness!
Even when their paths wind through the dark valley of tears,
they dig deep to find a pleasant pool where others find only pain.
He gives to them a brook of blessing filled from the rain of an
outpouring. They grow stronger and stronger with every step
forward, and the God of all gods will appear before them in Zion.

Psalm 84:5-7 (TPT)

it's not your fault

OUR BEDTIME ROUTINE was out of whack, so our son slept a little too long in one nappy. He had been bunking with us. Half-convenience, half-appeasing my anxiety, which peaked again since the miscarriage. After all, losing Shiloh was yet another reminder of how horrific things still happen, even though I know God has my family in his hands. Every time I wake during the night – which is a lot – I check to make sure our son's chest is rising and falling as it should.

So, this particular morning, when the poor thing woke up soaked through his pyjamas, I found myself immensely grateful I had turned off the electric blanket. He had even soaked through to the mattress protector.

Determined to know the legitimate severity of the what if scenarios racing through my mind, I started to google. I found a few articles warning against electric blankets. Use them to warm the bed, they wrote, then turn them off. Then, I came across an article that linked electric blankets to miscarriage. I couldn't read it. But I knew what if meant. Guilt overwhelmed me as I remembered the time when it was cold, I had been napping with my son, and I had left the blanket on...

I quickly became convinced the miscarriage was my fault, for leaving the electric blanket on that one time. I began to apologise to the Lord for taking his miracle for granted. I hadn't been as cautious as I was when I was pregnant with our son.

When I confessed this to my husband, however – fully ready to take responsibility for the loss of our precious one – he told it to me straight. 'It was not your fault. And I don't think reading articles like that is helpful.'

Tears welled in my eyes. 'I didn't read it as such.'

In this moment, I knew what I needed, and, praise Jesus, so did my husband. I didn't need a hug. I needed those redeeming words spoken over me.

'It wasn't your fault,' he said matter-of-factly.

I nodded. End of discussion. There was no need for confession, no need for apology. I had to come to terms with the fact that I wasn't to blame.

Because, in a way, it would be easier to lay blame on something tangible, something physical rather than the spiritual reality of a broken world where an enemy is set on derailing me from my calling and stealing my joy and trying to make me doubt God. It would be easier in some ways to blame myself. To say, 'I left the electric blanket on. It's my fault'... and then, in time, to add, 'I won't do that if God blesses us with another miracle...'

Of course, you can be sure, that electric blanket will be unplugged if I'm carrying another miracle in the future, just in case. But I can't blame it now. I can't blame myself either. It's not healthy and it's not true.

Fault falls on the shoulders of Satan, sin, and death. The moment Eve took and ate that fruit, the world as the Lord created it grew dark. Can you imagine for a moment? The moment fear and shame entered the world like a storm cloud. Adam and Eve, once at ease in each other's presence, hid and covered themselves in shame. The lion laying down by the lamb suddenly snarled and bared its teeth. Thorns began to choke vines. Birds scattered across the sky. Marsupials buried into the ground, hiding from predators. Animal turned against animal. Plants began to wither. The world began its slow deterioration that would last for thousands of years. Cain would commit the first murder, killing his brother Abel. And with that, Eve was not only the first woman but the first woman to lose a child. It's there, in the beginning. Abel would never be replaced in Eve's heart. But God did bless her with the consolation of another son, Seth.

We are human. We make mistakes. But the worst mistake we can make is giving ourselves too much credit and blame in this department because it lessens our need for God and His immeasurable grace. We need His grace over our lives. We need to know Jesus conquered Satan, sin, and death. That He is victorious. The battle is won, it's just a matter of time until He draws His saints to Himself for eternity.

We do not hold the balance of life in our hands, not even one life. Not our own. And certainly not our children's lives. As mothers, we do our best, but we need to rely on the Lord in our weakness. Only through Him do we have the strength to be a godly mother. Whether our children are in our earthly embrace or already in the arms of Jesus, we have been called to be godly mothers. And godly mothers know, deep down, that their children are on loan from God, whether it be for weeks, months, or years.

As the doctor said in that hospital room to me, 'There was nothing you could have done differently. This happens to 1 in 3 pregnancies. It's just not talked about enough...'

So I'm extending her words of consolation to you now. There was nothing you could have done differently. And the very fact that it's not talked about enough is why I am here, writing this book, praying that my words and the words of these grieving parents will assure you of the truth -

You are not alone.

You are not broken.

God is still good.

And if you've been beating yourself up with all the what if scenarios your imagination can conjure like I was, I beg you, put them to rest.

It's not your fault.

We know that the whole creation has been groaning as in the pains of childbirth right up to the present time. Not only so, but we ourselves, who have the firstfruits of the Spirit, groan inwardly as we wait eagerly for our adoption to sonship, the redemption of our bodies. For in this hope we were saved. But hope that is seen is no hope at all. Who hopes for what they already have? But if we hope for what we do not yet have, we wait for it patiently.

Romans 8:22-25

eternal promises

ONCE THE SHOCK began to settle, confusion festered. *How could a promised child die?* That certainly wasn't one for the storybooks.

My husband began to wonder whether I had been given two separate promises that morning. *You're pregnant... but then you're going to have a girl and call her Shiloh.*

It was a nice thought, but it wasn't one I could hold onto or resonate with. After all, I had prayed over my belly, whispering her name. I saw her heartbeat on the monitor. She was there. She existed. She couldn't just be the nameless predecessor of a rainbow daughter.

I wrestled with this and wondered how our daughter of promise could have been taken away. Then I remembered something my dad told me when he was in hospital for brain surgery, 'We hold this life too tightly,' he said as we sat on his hospital bed. Those words have stuck with me ever since. This life isn't all there is. In fact, it's not the best part by far.

Then I saw 'a new heaven and a new earth,' for the first heaven and the first earth had passed away, and there was no longer any sea. I saw the Holy City, the new Jerusalem, coming down out of heaven from God, prepared as a bride beautifully dressed for her husband.

And I heard a loud voice from the throne saying, 'Look! God's dwelling place is now among the people, and He will dwell with them. They will be His people, and God Himself will be with them and be their God. 'He will wipe every tear from their eyes. There will be no more death' or mourning or crying or pain, for the old order of things has passed away... I did not see a temple in the city, because the Lord God Almighty and the Lamb are its temple. The city does not need the sun or the moon to shine on it, for the glory of God gives it light, and the Lamb is its lamp.

Revelation 21: 1-4,22-23

Maybe, just maybe, Shiloh was always intended to be in the dwelling place of God, just like the meaning of her name? And maybe, her name was a gift, not just prophesying of her place in God's eternal Kingdom, but as a testament to His faithfulness?

Because I will be forever grateful that we have a name to grieve and speak out loud.

I am also grateful that the first thing our sweet baby girl saw was the face of Jesus. All she knows is His Love and Light.

So, promised or not, our daughter Shiloh didn't miss out on anything by not stopping by in this world first before skipping ahead to our true home. When we lose loved ones to death in this world, we can begin to use phrases like, 'At least they aren't suffering anymore' or 'It was their time... their time was *up'*. No, their time was only just beginning. Outside of time, no less. (Or however that works in heaven)

Let us not mistake our grief and sadness with pity for our children or any loved one who we deemed slipped away too soon. As the old adage goes, *it's not you, it's me*. In this case, it's us. *We* are the ones who have missed out on spending this short life with our child. But the beautiful part is that this short life isn't all there is. We cannot even comprehend the beauty that awaits us in our true home. We weren't created for a broken world, that's why God worked so hard to redeem us and draw us back to Himself through Jesus. Our God is holy. He created us to live in relationship with Him. And one day, that relationship will become fully known to us as we bask in His majestic presence and the light of His glory ignites the faces of our loved ones waiting for us.

*For this world is not our permanent home;
we are looking forward to a home yet to come.*

Hebrews 13:14 (NLT)

a sound mind

IN LATE 2020, I was diagnosed with severe post-partum stress, anxiety, and depression. Just hearing those words made me feel ungrateful for the precious gift of my son. It made me feel like a failure and – with the thought of therapy – a crazy person.

As it turns out, there was underlying trauma from an attempted break-in years prior that I hadn't dealt with, hence why I began imagining intruders during the night. I had conjured them up so completely I could even tell you now what their imaginary faces looked like. What I didn't realise was how something as simple as Cognitive Behavioural Therapy could draw me out of that emotional headspace and help me to think logically about the potential threat and whether it was legitimate. But, in the darkest moments, when CBT wouldn't even work, all I could rely on was prayer and Psalm 127.

> *Unless the LORD builds the house,*
> *The builders labour in vain.*
> *Unless the LORD watches over the city,*
> *The guards stand watch in vain.*
> *In vain you rise early*
> *And stay up late,*
> *Toiling for food to eat –*
> *For He grants sleep to those He loves.*
>
> Psalm 127:1-2

Sometimes this Psalm was the only thing that would force me to stop listening to the house and finally rest. It has been a long journey through anxiety but once I began to apply lessons from therapy through the lens of God's Word my fear subsided like a temporary tide. But there is one sure way to reignite one's fear, so it rages even stronger than before. Tragedy. Tragedy acts as the reminder that bad things *do* happen. Our God is Sovereign but that does not make us immune to suffering. In fact, the Christian life screams the opposite. We are told in God's Word that we can expect to suffer.

Therefore, since we have been justified through faith, we have peace with God through our Lord Jesus Christ, through whom we have gained access by faith into this grace in which we now stand. And we boast in the hope of the glory of God. Not only so, but we also glory in our sufferings, because we know that suffering produces perseverance; perseverance character; and character, hope. And hope does not put us to shame, because God's love has been poured out into our hearts through the Holy Spirit, who has been given to us.

Romans 5:1-5

I often tell people that if it wasn't for my tumultuous past, I wouldn't understand the beautiful all-consuming grace and love of God. I can now say, if it wasn't for *this* suffering – the loss of our precious baby – I could not have experienced Jesus in such an intimate way. I am forever changed not only because of the new empathy I have for fellow mothers who are also navigating this grief, but because of the closeness of God and His divine faithfulness, it is incomparable to anything I have ever experienced.

Agnes Beaumont wrote, '*I have often observed the more trouble I have had, either from within or without, the more I have found God's presence, when I have been helped to keep close to him by frequent fervent prayer, and – O! how sweet is his presence to a poor soul, when surrounded by sorrows on every side... It cannot be expressed what sweetness there is in his presence, and in one promise applied by his Spirit to the soul...*

For my part I can say with David, I have found trouble and sorrow... But, on the other hand, none knows, but God, that sweet communion and consolation which he hath graciously offered me, in those hours of trouble. I have experienced such comfort and enlargement of heart, such fervent desires after Christ and his grace, as hath often made me thank God for trouble, because I found it drove me nearer to himself, and the throne of his grace. The Lord has made such seasons praying, heart-searching, and soul-humbling times.'

And just as the Lord drew near in a vision to comfort me, He also used the words of Agnes Beaumont, a seventeenth century woman who I had little in common with aside from our faith. Then again, perhaps that's the most important part, to be sisters in Christ across generational divides. God used the words of this woman long gone into eternity to comfort me.

I still experience acute paralysing fear. Like grief, it is something I must navigate rather than conquer. But when it strikes, I speak 2 Timothy 1:7 over myself and remember that God did not give me a spirit of fear – and if it doesn't come from Him, then there's only one other place. But the Spirit of God gives me power, love, and a sound mind.

And He wants to give that to you too.

Claim it.

Speak it.

For God has not given us a spirit of fear,
but of power and of love and of a sound mind.

2 Timothy 1:7 (NKJV)

two daughters

I ONCE DREAMT I had two daughters. The elder had auburn hair, she was tall like me, fair with freckles and pale eyes. The younger was darker with a round face, my blue eyes, her daddy's long dark lashes, and a rosebud mouth. The two of them were playing by this enormous unlit fireplace in a castle where the women of our family had gathered with their daughters. There was a four-poster bed where some of my cousins sat chatting happily. I don't remember any of the conversations, only my two daughters being there.

Prior to this dream, my husband and I made the decision to remove the Implanon from my arm and to go sans-contraception. For me, the Implanon dramatically messed with my cycle, and I wanted some regularity. We were also very open to the possibility of starting our family within the next year or so.

It's funny, when I had it removed, I distinctly remember the Holy Spirit telling me to wait until my cycle rebooted to start trying. In that moment, however, I disregarded it as a weird thought rather than God trying to warn me. I had ovulation pains soon after the removal. So, I didn't wait, which left me wondering whether or not my period was going to start. The doctor said it would come within the week. It didn't. Instead, I received a faint positive pregnancy test.

Now, to put this day into context, I had prayed for a positive so I could tell my grandmother, who was in hospital, before she died. If it was a girl, I wanted her to be her namesake, for she was a great prayer warrior.

My grandmother was the first person to know. Then she told my mum who later cornered me, grinning in the hospital carpark, and talking to my flat stomach.

Once when I visited the hospital, my grandmother told me to give the baby our names as its middle name. If the baby was a boy, he would have my husband's name. And if she was a girl, she would have mine. I was confident in that moment I had a little Raiya Elizabeth growing in me. After all, with the early positive and my grandmother slowly passing into eternity to be with 'her Jesus', it just felt right.

I was almost eight weeks at her funeral. I already had the first trimester bloat, only, when I went to the doctor to double check everything, my HCG levels weren't high enough to confirm pregnancy. A week later, at work, I began to bleed.

At the time, I wondered if it had all been in my head. The uncertainty of it all made me doubt everything. Though, looking back now, I know it was real. She existed. Because now I know what pregnancy feels like. The bleeding had just felt like a heavy period, but I just knew I was pregnant. I just knew. Later, when talking to another mother, she helped me feel a little less crazy. 'Yeah, you just know... we even had a few negative tests at first, but I just knew...'

When I think back, Raiya must have been so fleeting my body had to catch up with what was happening. But she was there.

> *I'm sleeping on my stomach*
> *I'm slouching in the chair*
> *I need to feel your absence*
> *It tells me you were there*
> *That old familiar tightness*
> *The swelling of my breast*
> *Discomfort, sweet discomfort*
> *Like breath caught in my chest*
> *You must be someone special*
> *Our little Baby Girl*
> *If God already took you*
> *Out of this broken world*

It would take two more years to fall pregnant with our son. Then almost a year and a half later with Shiloh.

It's strange how in my dream I didn't see my son. Then again, maybe it was because God knew I would never get to see my daughters' faces in this world, and He gave me that gift. Maybe, those two daughters are my heavenly children, waiting for me patiently, nestled on Jesus' lap, waiting for Mummy to finally come home.

*He gives the barren woman a home,
making her the joyous mother of children.
Praise the Lord!*

Psalm 113:9 (ESV)

restoration

UNBEKNOWNST TO ME, I was raised in the shadows of infant loss. Back when I was barely a toddler myself, a lovely Christian family invited our family over for dinner one night and, while we were there, their daughter passed away to SIDS.

Mum described it to me years later and confessed that she had been more hysterical in the moment than her dear friend fighting for her daughter's life. Paranoia then seeped into Mum's own maternal ways as she raised me.

After Shiloh went to be with the Lord, I saw this life-long family friend at a birthday party. In the sacred space that exists between bereaved mothers, I told her of my loss. She gazed at me, her eyes brimming with empathy, and told me what had encouraged her after the unimaginable happened.

As Christians, we are familiar with the story of Job and are encouraged to take comfort that there is a reason behind suffering and that there is a spiritual battle raging around us every moment. In the story of Job, we watch him lose everything and then we see God restore it, but not without clarifying Who God is and what He has done. One part of this story that I hadn't noticed – which this dear woman of God shared with me this night – was that Job's livestock and riches were doubled when God restored them, however, Job was given the same number of children once again.

After Job had prayed for his friends, the LORD restored his fortunes and gave him twice as much as he had before. All his brothers and sisters and everyone who had known him before came and ate with him in his house. They comforted and consoled him over all the trouble the LORD had brought on him, and each one gave him a piece of silver and a gold ring. The LORD blessed the latter part of Job's life more than the former part. He had fourteen thousand sheep, six thousand camels, a thousand yoke of oxen and a thousand donkeys. And he also had seven sons and three daughters.

Job 42:10-12

I had never given this much thought, but God gave Job the same number of children because that *was* double the restoration. Job now had seven sons and three daughters in heaven, and he had seven sons and three daughters on the earth. Once he and his family passed into eternity, he would have twenty children to call him 'Dad'.

By God's grace, this godly woman went on to have three daughters and a son. Thirty-something years later, she maintains the hope of meeting her heavenly daughter one day.

*He said, 'Naked (without possessions) I came [into this world] from
my mother's womb, and naked I will return there.
The Lord gave and the Lord has taken away;
Blessed be the name of the Lord.'
Through all this Job did not sin nor did he blame God.*

Job 1:21-22 (AMP)

love & prayers

THE SADDEST FUNERAL WE EVER ATTENDED was that of a most beloved yet stillborn son. What shattered me was the size of the white casket. I wasn't sure what I expected, but seeing that casket covered with a blue baby blanket and crafts made by elder siblings just made me want to hug my son all the tighter.

To this day, I remain completely in awe of the strength of that family, especially of that mother, a dear friend of ours. This was my prayer for them that day and it is my prayer for you, dear reader...

Heavenly Father,

Thank You that we can come to Your throne of grace with confidence, knowing You are a God who loves and listens and draws near to the broken hearted.

We ask now for Your peace that transcends all understanding to rest on this family – today, tomorrow and always – as they remember the loss of their child.

We know Your ways are higher than our own. Though we cannot comprehend or understand why You brought this child home so soon, we know that You have this beautiful family in Your loving hands and that they are part of Your Kingdom plan.

Still, we ask for the comfort of Your Holy Spirit to especially be with this mother and father as they mourn their precious child. We know there is still hope and that this goodbye is only temporary - as much as it is deeply felt now – and that one day we will be reunited with this child in eternity. In the place You have prepared for those who love You, a place free from tears and pain and death.

Thank You that You gave Your Son, Jesus Christ, so that this may be made possible through his sacrifice. Father, You have this child in Your arms now. We just pray that Your embrace would extend to all those mourning.

We pray through the Holy Spirit and in the precious and mighty name of Jesus Christ our Saviour,

Amen.

Your friend went to heaven before you could play.
Before your friend even knew his own name,
it was written in the Lamb's Book of Life.
When your friend went to heaven, you saw us cry
and pray on the phone with his daddy that night.
None of us can fathom the reason why –
your friend went to heaven.

in memory of Micah James
June 2021

*Brothers and sisters, we do not want you to be uninformed about
those who sleep in death, so that you do not grieve
like the rest of mankind, who have no hope.*

1 Thessalonians 4:13

speak it

SUNDAY MORNINGS WERE HARD with a toddler as it was, let alone trying to parent and be present at church on my own. Still, if my husband was home with a migraine then I would still take our son to church, even if it meant staying in the parents' room the whole time.

My husband prayed over us, as he does each morning, but during his prayer had a slip of the tongue. It could have been the migraine. It could have been any number of things. But in his prayer, he committed each of us to the Lord, including Shiloh.

The mention of her name startled me at first. But it was like the sudden application of restoring ointment, swiftly acting as a balm for my soul.

He had said her name.

No one said her name.

Of course, I was acutely aware of her and her name. She had grown inside me. She tragically died inside me. And now I had the daily physical representation of her memory in a keepsake box beside my bed, where her cradle would have been. Her name was engraved on the top along with the words *forever in the dwelling place of God.*

So, I was so aware of her name.

I just didn't think anyone else was.

My husband kissed us – our son and I – then went inside and I drove to church remembering the sound of her name.

What was *your* child's name?

If you haven't named them, I would encourage you to do so and write their name in the back of this book on the 'honouring' page.

Because there is something healing about speaking it.

Because they existed here on earth – albeit briefly – within you. And now they exist in another realm where they are free from the burdens of sin.

Because quite often we suffer in silence because we don't have a name to speak or a casket to cry over.

I smile when I look at the keepsake box beside my bed. Yes, within it there are sympathy cards and dried flowers. But, for me, those words on the front of the box fill me with hope –

forever in the dwelling place of God.

And if you have faith in Jesus, one day you will go to that place and meet your little one. He or she will call you 'Mama' and then you'll probably get to meet their guardian angel who stepped up to watch over them at the command of King Jesus.

If, by some chance, this book has made it into your hands and you don't know Jesus as your Lord and Saviour – can I encourage you to reach out to Him? He alone is the reason any of this makes sense. He alone can redeem our grief. He alone can turn ashes into beauty, mourning into overwhelming joy. He alone is the Way, the Truth, and the Life.

And He is the reason our children are safe now in paradise.

*Jesus answered, 'I am the Way, the Truth, and the Life.
No one comes to the Father except through me.'*

John 14:6

the phoenix

EVERYTHING CHANGED.
A definitive moment in history transformed the person I once recognised in the mirror. I still saw glimpses of her sometimes. But this new person was significantly different. Changed. Marked. There was life before 5 September 2021 and there was life after. The loss. The trauma. The grief. Those change a person.

Like a phoenix bird, the old me faded to ash and a new person emerged – a stronger mother yet simultaneously depleted from loss.

But *why*?

Why *this* experience?

Tragically, with much of secular culture embracing the legalisation of abortion, the world has become desensitised to the value of human life in the womb. The results have been devastatingly tragic. Pregnancy loss has been inadvertently affected, as much of the world believes *it* wasn't even a baby yet but an embryo or foetus or other scientific term used to dehumanise our children.

I remember when I first saw my son's heartbeat pulse on the ultrasound screen. He was nine weeks in utero. At sixteen weeks, he started kicking and only became more active, rolling around, as the weeks went on. At twenty weeks, his ultrasound photo was perfectly clear with his button nose and pronounced chin. While he was still inside me, lullabies settled his heartrate in the hospital when the nurse was trying to take our observations.

To think of anything happening to him during this vulnerable time in his life sickens me to the core.

But the enemy has twisted something that God created to be beautiful to be seen as a limitation on women's rights and freedom. It is this mindset that has meant mothers are expected to 'get over' their loss, because it's not valid.

Only, it *is*.

Every single child – whether in utero, on the earth, or in heaven – is significant.

That's why this loss is so devastating.

Our child was taken. All the dreams of a future in this world we held for them was taken. It's against the natural order of life. It's not right. It's not the way God intended it to be. And He's planning a beautiful family reunion for us in eternity.

But, for now, for us here on earth, everything has changed.

Therefore, having been justified by faith, we have peace with God through our Lord Jesus Christ, through whom also we have access by faith into this grace in which we stand, and rejoice in hope of the glory of God. And not only that, but we also glory in tribulations, knowing that tribulation produces perseverance; and perseverance, character; and character, hope. Now hope does not disappoint, because the love of God has been poured out in our hearts by the Holy Spirit who was given to us.

Romans 5:1-5 (NKJV)

sacred space

I SWIFTLY LEARNED THERE WAS NOTHING anyone could say to relieve the pain. Even if I managed to say 'thank you' to their 'I'm so sorry for your loss' – rather than the obligatory 'it's okay' (because it isn't) – even then, if the exchange went as needed, there was little more to say. Because this specific type of grief is often silent. It's complex. People don't know what to say. We don't know what we need. I didn't know what to ask for because I didn't know what would help. That was until I spoke to a counsellor.

I had reached the end of myself. I clung to my faith but I knew I needed help resurfacing from this deep consuming place. What I didn't know was that I needed a space to grieve. I needed a space to be fragile. I needed a space to celebrate Shiloh in heaven, to recognise her by name and know that she is perfect now, in eternity, sitting by Jesus' feet. I needed someone to hold that space for me, to allow me to enter in, to allow me to cry, to be angry, to share my deepest fears.

What I didn't realise was how much I needed this counselling for so many reasons seemingly unrelated and yet all connected. Events in my childhood, adult decisions, it all began to surface as I worked through these complex emotions of guilt and shame. Why did I feel like I failed? Where did that come from? Why did I sometimes, in the darkest parts of me, believe I was being punished by God?

All these questions I began to wrestle with. I'd walk away exhausted with splotches of mascara on my face but with slightly straighter shoulders that weren't as weighed down as they used to be. Each week I would collapse into my bed with a throbbing headache. Sometimes I'd cry a little, but mostly out of relief. And in prayer. I would ask God to bring healing to these broken places unearthed in this sacred space.

Because that is what it is. Sacred. As I write this, I've finished my Wednesday session and discovered a new way to deal with the cry headaches – water, Panadol, and a thermal eye mask. And of course, bed.

Because this is also a sacred space. It's where I can give my worries over to God. I can rest here beside the keepsake box with Shiloh's name engraved upon it and remember that she is with Jesus. She's alive. And one day, I will meet her.

During my first counselling session, I described this keepsake box and all that was in it. Sympathy cards, dried flowers, candle, ultrasound photo...

'Why is her photo in a box?'

It was a fair question. Why, in my grief, did I think I had to hide her away? Even if she did look like a jellybean. She was my jellybean. With a flashing heartbeat. She was our daughter.

First thing I did when I left that session was buy a photo frame. Her ultrasound photo now sits on the shelf by my bed, next to the grayscale photo of her brother.

It's a sacred space. A space held for photos of my children, near and far, to remind me of the grace of God and the fact that I have a daughter and I will hold space for her memory and look forward to the day when we are reunited.

The children born during your bereavement
will yet say in your hearing,
'This place is too small for us;
give us more space to live in.'

Isaiah 49:20

ready? set? no.

THREE MONTHS AFTER LOSING SHILOH, I was still counting the weeks I would've been pregnant. I imagined how big my second trimester belly would have been, I imagined being pregnant at Christmas and all the joy that came with that season. But I wasn't pregnant. Not anymore. And if I was really honest with myself, I wasn't ready to be pregnant again either.

It all came to a head when my two-week wait turned into a faint line on a pregnancy test. An evaporation line that eventuated from having a toddler accompanying me to the bathroom and me having to swiftly stow my test away in my dressing gown. I found it the following morning to discover that half line. The line every woman trying to conceive wants to see. Only, we weren't trying. But we weren't *not* trying either.

A few days later I received a Big Fat Negative followed by my period. And I was left reeling. Because...

I was relieved.

Which made me question *everything*.

Guilt struck once again, the way it likes to, bringing me down and making me fight against my better judgement. I resolved that I didn't want to be pregnant which meant I didn't want a baby which must have meant I hadn't really wanted Shiloh...

Round and round it went. Guilt. Confusion. Grief.

I took these emotions into my next counselling session and laid them on the table. There, in the warm light of that sacred space, I could see things more clearly.

I *had* wanted Shiloh. So desperately. So completely that I still wasn't ready to let her go.

And that was okay.

I wasn't ready for a rainbow baby. I wasn't ready to try to give our son a sibling.

My husband in all his beautiful patience and wisdom understood and agreed completely and we went from 'not trying' to *preventing.*

I went back on the pill. For a season. However long that needed to be.

Again, I felt lighter. I didn't have the two-week wait. I didn't feel the pressure to move forward. I could just be in this place. Decidedly *not ready.*

And I will wait until the desire returns. I will wait until hope is restored and rises so greatly that I have peace about moving forward and planning a new pregnancy. But that moment is not now.

Not yet.

*Hope deferred makes the heart sick,
but a longing fulfilled is a tree of life.*

Proverbs 13:12

songs in the night

I REMEMBER THE DAY we lost Raiya – our first loss with so many question marks lingering over it, causing me to doubt my body and my own sanity. I remember clutching the steering wheel as I drove home from work, bleeding, tears flooding my eyes, anger burning in my heart, and singing the only hymn I knew by heart.

> *'When peace like a river attendeth my way*
> *When sorrow when sea billows roll*
> *Whatever my lot, thou hast taught me to say*
> *"It is well, it is well with my soul"*

The writer of this hymn, Horatio Spafford, knew what it was to lose a child. During a time of financial turmoil, his four-year-old son died of scarlet fever. Then, believing his family needed a vacation, his wife and four daughters travelled by ship to England with the understanding that Horatio would later join them after he finished his business at home. Tragically, the ship collided and sunk, claiming the lives of Horatio's four daughters. Only his wife Anna survived. Upon receiving a telegram beginning with the words, *'Saved alone. What shall I do'*, Horatio set sail for England.

> *'On Thursday last we passed over the spot where she went down in mid-ocean, the water three miles deep. But I do not think of our dear ones there. They are safe, folded, the dear lambs, and there, before very long, shall we be too. In the meantime, thanks to God, we have an opportunity to serve and praise Him for His love and mercy to us and ours. I will praise Him while I have my being.*
> *May we each one arise, leave all, and follow Him.'*
>
> Horatio Spafford, 1873

And so, Horatio Spafford wrote his song in the night that would later comfort this grieving mother and thousands of others across the world.

Can you remember your songs in the night? If your heart can't put it into words, will you turn with me to a song in God's Word? Will you open your Bible and pray Psalm 77 out loud?

In his commentary on this passage, Matthew Henry wrote that *'drooping saints, that are of a sorrowful spirit, may here as in a glass see their faces...'*

Will you look into the mirror? And once you have, will you remember your songs in the night?

My mind wandered, thinking of days gone by
The years long since passed.
Then I remembered the worship songs
I used to sing in the night seasons,
And my heart began to fill again with thoughts of you.
So my spirit went out once more in search of you.

Psalm 77:5-6

No matter what lies the enemy has tried to whisper to you in the middle of the night, in those moments when he tries to claim your sleep with fear and grief. No matter what tricks he pulls on you, remember your songs in the night. Remember that Jesus is victorious. He is Sovereign. And though Satan should strike, battle, and buffet us. Though trials threaten to overwhelm us. We have this blessed assurance. That Christ is strong when we are weak. He looks upon our hopelessness and helplessness and makes a way to redeem us. No matter what we've done or haven't done, it is nailed to His cross and we bear it no more. With this truth, we must argue ourselves down from the ledge of the darkest depths of grief.

'Despondency of spirit, and distrust of God, under affliction, are too often the infirmities of good people. When at any time it is working in us we must suppress the rising of it. We must argue down the insurrections of unbelief.'

Matthew Henry

We can't do this in our own strength. The hope that is in us comes from God and God alone. But may He haste the day when our faith – and His hope and love – shall be sight. When the clouds be rolled back as a scroll. The trumpet shall resound. The Lord shall descend. A song in the night, oh my soul...

Yet I could never forget all your miracles, my God,
as I remember all your wonders of old.

Psalm 77:11 (TPT)

soon

WHEN THE STARS ALIGN and our little man falls asleep on-time and in his own bed, my husband and I watch *The Chosen*. I enjoy this show for so many reasons, but one part I found amusing was the in-joke around the word 'soon'. When Simon-Peter becomes impatient for greater things and urges the Lord to give him more information *soon*, Jesus tells him to ask his Father in Heaven what *soon* really means. Likewise, when Jesus talks to John the Baptiser about *soon*, they share a knowing smile.

If you're anything like me, I wanted to physically heal *soon*. I wanted to stop crying *soon*. I wanted to want my rainbow baby *soon* but seemed to battle guilt all the more whenever I considered it. And I wanted that guilt gone yesterday, if not *sooner*.

But God isn't limited to our human clock, and some things are far more precious when we journey with Him and give up all ideas about *soon*.

> *But do not forget this one thing, dear friends:*
> *With the Lord a day is like a thousand years,*
> *and a thousand years are like a day.*

2 Peter 3:8

It can feel like He is inactive in the waiting, but there is an intimacy with Jesus to be experienced in that place of waiting and hoping, like clinging to the hem of His garment, knowing that something is coming. Healing. Hope. Health.

> *...but those who hope in the LORD*
> *will renew their strength.*
> *They will soar on wings like eagles;*
> *They will run and not grow weary,*
> *They will walk and not be faint.*

Isaiah 40:31

Does He feel near or far to you right now? As you read this, does He feel tangible, or distant?

> *This is what the LORD says to me:*
> *'I will remain quiet and will look on from my dwelling place,*
> *Like shimmering heat in the sunshine,*
> *Like a cloud of dew in the heat of harvest.*

Isaiah 18:4

Even if it feels like God is quiet, He's there. He's in that small thing that makes you smile, even if it's just for a moment. He's in that worship song that you feel was written just for you. He's in the Bible verse leaping off the page and into your heart. He's in that hug from a friend. He's in that text from a loved one, letting you know you're on their mind.

He's in *this* book.

And He's waiting for the exact moment to meet you where you are. His timing is perfect. Even when we, like Simon-Peter, can be impatient for life to fall into place the way we expect. Jesus said He is coming *soon* and two thousand years later, we're still waiting. And we have to be okay with that.

God is patient. It's in His very identity. God is love (1 Jn 4:16) and love is patient (1 Cor. 13:4). It's the very first description in that passage on love. Patient. Long-Suffering. Fore-bearing.

And soon, Jesus will introduce us to our little ones in heaven. We just need to be patient. Our children are not lost. They're safe. They're waiting for us to come home.

I imagine my little Shiloh Grace sitting on the knee of her Heavenly Father, asking, 'Are they here yet?'

'Not yet,' He tells her gently, '*soon*.'

He who testified to these things says,
'Yes, I am coming soon.'
Amen. Come, Lord Jesus.

Revelation 22:20

a fable of hope

ONCE UPON A TIME, in a realm far from the laws that bind our own, there lived Evangeline. She breathed. Her heart continued to beat. Even when it felt like it should stop. After all, the enemy had stolen Treasure, her precious baby, and he had taken her to a place Evangeline could not follow.

There was only One who could venture there, only One who could rescue Treasure from a life devoid of light and love.

The Prince of Light.

Evangeline had tried with all her strength to defend Treasure, to keep her safe, to search for her even after she had been taken. But to no avail. No, she knew she would not survive the enemy's void, there was only One strong enough to conquer the enemy and save Treasure.

The Prince of Light.

And He was there, right beside her, wanting to help her. Only Evangeline's cries were so loud, her sorrow so deep, that she couldn't hear His gentle voice.

She searched for Him. She journeyed over the Rageous Mountains, cursing the jagged road beneath her feet so loudly, she could not hear the Prince of Light's voice guiding her to softer ground. She battled through the Blamesome Woods, where the spiked boughs cut her skin and tree roots tripped her up. This time she became so paranoid that when the Prince of Light tried to take her hand, she flinched away in fear. Evangeline swam through the Tremoring River, where the icy water turned her numb, so numb she couldn't feel the Prince of Light's presence. She reached the bank where Weeping Willows joined her song of the night, their branches wailing through the air so aggressively they knocked her off her feet. There, exhausted, wounded, frozen, lonely, wretched, and guilt-ridden, Evangeline finally heard His gentle call.

'Dear one, come here,' He said with tears in His immense eyes. 'Let me carry you.'

She fell into His arms.

One by one He saw to her wounds. He warmed her with His embrace. He sang over her a song of hope then told her of all that had come to pass.

'I caught the enemy when he tried to steal Treasure and I rescued her.'

'Then where is she?' Evangeline asked.

'Dear one,' He began, 'you know how special Treasure is.'

'I do. Of course, I do.'

'Treasure is so special, I wanted her to be safe forever.'

'I want that too,' Evangeline said. 'So where is she?'

'She is in the safest place I know. A castle in my Father's Eternal Kingdom where the enemy can never harm her again.'

Evangeline breathed deeply, steadying her frantic heart. 'Can I see her?'

'Soon,' He promised. 'But for now, I still have a plan and purpose for you here. Then, when the time is right, I will take you there as well.'

'How can your plan and purpose be greater than me being with Treasure?'

'You may not understand now,' said the Prince of Light, 'but one day you will. One day it will all make sense. One day you will join Treasure in that place of safety and the enemy will be no more.'

'Do you promise?'

The Prince of Light gazed at her lovingly. 'I promise.'

Then I saw 'a new heaven and a new earth,' for the first heaven and the first earth had passed away, and there was no longer any sea. I saw the Holy City, the new Jerusalem, coming down out of heaven from God, prepared as a bride beautifully dressed for her husband. And I heard a loud voice from the throne saying,
'Look! God's dwelling place is now among the people, and he will dwell with them. They will be his people, and God himself will be with them and be their God. 'He will wipe every tear from their eyes. There will be no more death' or mourning or crying or pain, for the old order of things has passed away.'

He who was seated on the throne said, 'I am making everything new!' Then he said, 'Write this down, for these words are trustworthy and true.'

He said to me: 'It is done. I am the Alpha and the Omega, the Beginning and the End. To the thirsty I will give water without cost from the spring of the water of life. Those who are victorious will inherit all this, and I will be their God and they will be my children.'

Revelation 21:1-7

testimonies

to the bereaved mother

by Stephanie Richmond

You keep hearing, 'let me know if you need anything,' and you're extremely grateful for the sentiment. But somewhere deep in your heart, it's really, really hard to embrace these words.

It's hard because you don't know what you need or want. The pain is just too much – an avalanche of emotions that suffocates your very breath within.

It's as though the wound is much deeper than you ever thought it could be – a heartache – a groaning too deep for words.

Oh, how wonderful it would be to have a friend not only tell you with their words but tell you with their heartfelt actions, too.

I'm far from perfect or from getting it *right*, but maybe, just maybe I can help remind you that I'm here with you...

Maybe you don't want me to come inside, let alone come over, but let me leave this food at your doorstep.

Maybe you aren't ready to come over to my house either, but let me invite you to my weekend BBQ, still.

Maybe you'll say 'no,' to all the invites, but let me keep trying to include you.

Maybe you don't want to talk on the phone, or you're fearful about the platitudes, but let me leave this prayer on your voicemail.

Maybe you can't bring yourself to text me back, or you're hesitant about asking for help, but let me check on you daily, still.

Maybe you're just too tired and too worn to wash your face or your hair – let me send you some dry shampoo and facial cleansing wipes anyway.

Maybe you don't want the lights on while you cry silently, but let me send you this candle to give you a little flicker of hope.

Maybe you don't want your beloved child to be forgotten, so let me help keep their memory alive.

Maybe in this very moment, you're struggling with little faith, but let me wrap you in words from Him.

Maybe you just don't know how to be...

You see, I don't know exactly what you need or want. But I wholeheartedly know that I don't want you to ever feel alone. I want to be in the trenches of grief with you – not just with my words but with my actions, too.

I want to help shoulder the pain and remind you in word and deed...

You and your family are valued. Y'all are loved. And I'll never stop praying for the Prince of Peace to comfort y'all with the kind of peace that surpasses all understanding.

Maybe, just maybe, we can get through this together.

xo soul-knitted friend

P.S. No matter how silent you may get,
I'll never leave you alone in your suffering.

my babies

by Josie Green

We were nearing the end of 2020: the year that made history with COVID-19 and the divisive presidential election. Especially for me, a registered nurse working on the inpatient floors of my hospital, it had been a rough year. As we reached the last months of 2020 we were just hoping and praying 2021 would be better, and things would return to normal. So imagine our joy when on November 3rd, 2020 I missed my period and took a pregnancy test which quickly turned positive. We had not been trying for a baby, but we weren't NOT trying either. We were so excited for this glimmer of hope coming out of 2020. We planned to tell our families at Christmas. Unfortunately, our joy was short lived. December 9th, the day before my scheduled ultrasound, I started spotting red. I just knew in my momma's heart I was having a miscarriage. I continued spotting the next day, a little heavier now. That afternoon, around 2 pm, my husband drove me to my scheduled ultrasound. Due to COVID, he was not allowed in, but he wanted to be as close as he could be. I knew in my heart this ultrasound was going to bring bad news, but I was trying to hold onto hope. The ultrasound tech did an abdominal ultrasound, then a transvaginal one. All I could see was an empty sac measuring 6w6d. I was supposed to be 9w4d. She barely said a word to me. Didn't answer my questions, just told me the radiologist would review the scan and then send it to my OB office. Being a nurse, I knew what I was seeing. I was sure on my dates, I knew my baby was gone. I walked out of the hospital numb, everything around me was blurry like in the movies. We went home and my husband helped me into bed and I stayed there for the rest of the day. I didn't eat, I didn't sleep. I couldn't understand why God would let this happen, this year of all years. My husband went to work the next morning, neither of us realising what that day would be like. Around 9 or 10 am, I woke up bleeding and in severe pain. I texted my husband and he turned around and drove the 90 minutes home to be with me. The pain was horrible, unlike anything I had felt before. My body was in labor, trying to deliver the baby who was no longer there. I wanted to die, the pain was so bad. After trying for hours to get a hold of my OB, she finally called back. Very sympathetic, she said that the blood loss was normal and it should slow down soon. She prescribed Tramadol for me for the pain, as I had been in excruciating pain for 6 hours at this point. A couple hours later the pain and bleeding began to subside a bit. I still didn't get out of bed that day except to go to the bathroom, and didn't eat. The next day, I did get up to eat something, and frosted Christmas cookies that night as I needed to do something normal for a little while. My mom stopped over to see us, and gave me a crayon drawing of a lamb in memory of our little Timothy. I had had a strong feeling that our baby was a boy, and Timothy was the name we had chosen if he was indeed a boy, so it made perfect sense to keep calling him Timothy. Just days before we miscarried, I had seen a post from one of my acquaintances across the country about how she had miscarried her baby in November. I reached out to her a couple days after we miscarried, and she was one of the reasons I got through the next days and weeks and months.

Even through our deep sorrow and loss, we did realise that God is still good. He did not want our baby to die, but because of all the sin in the world, He did allow it. He could have stopped it, He could have made our baby grow, but He did not. We may never understand why God works the way He does, but through it all, He is still good. It was ok for us to be angry, to question Him. He understood. We knew our baby Timothy was with Jesus. My favorite quote I got on a necklace after this was *'To think when you opened your tiny little eyes the first person you saw was Jesus'*. I ordered an ornament as well with his name and heavenly birthday on it.

After my first period in January, we started trying again. We missed our little boy so much but knew we wanted a baby. A few months passed with negative tests each month. Until April. April 1st, two days before my period was due, I got a very faint positive. I didn't have much hope for this one, as the line was barely visible and I was spotting lightly. Over the next couple days I got slightly darker lines, which were definitely positive, but not as dark as they should have been. My OB ordered HCG levels, but there was an issue with the transmission between the office and the lab and the lab couldn't find them Saturday morning, April 3rd, when I went to have them drawn. We ended up in the ER that night as I had begun bleeding a little more and I desperately wanted my bloodwork done. My HCG came back as 6, and nothing was seen on ultrasound, which could be perfectly normal for 4 weeks. They diagnosed me with a 'threatened abortion' and told me to come back if I started cramping as they couldn't rule out an ectopic pregnancy. We told our families again we were experiencing what would probably end up being another miscarriage. The next day was Easter. I stayed home from church as I didn't really feel like going out, and we didn't go to my parents for Easter dinner. I started cramping that afternoon, just on one side, and we went back to the ER that evening. HCG was 4, ultrasound was still nonconclusive, and I left with a script for another HCG level the next day. I knew an HCG of 4 is considered pre-pregnancy levels and knew we had had a 'chemical pregnancy' and lost another baby. My level the next day remained 4. I saw my OB that day who confirmed that yes I had had a second miscarriage and did more bloodwork to see if we could find a cause. This loss didn't really sink in until later in the week. I had barely had time to find out I was pregnant, and knew right away there probably wasn't much hope, and then days later knew I was miscarrying. We had no idea if this baby was a girl or a boy, so we gave baby a gender neutral name, Morgan. In the weeks to come, I would develop a strong feeling this baby was a girl, so she is now a girl in my heart. I ordered an ornament in memory of her with her name and heavenly birthday on it, and my mom drew me another lamb picture in memory of her. I bled for a few days, more just like a period as it was such an early miscarriage.

 A few months went by, and then on August 17th, I got a faint positive a week before my period was due. I had immediate bloodwork and progesterone was added to help support this pregnancy and I am now 18 weeks with this 3rd baby. But even though I now have a 3rd baby on the way, does not mean I miss my other babies any less. I still cry for them, I am sobbing right now as I write this. Being pregnant again doesn't lessen the pain of the ones I lost before. Yes, the pain changes, but it doesn't go away. But I want to encourage you, do not give up hope. After we lost Timothy, I wanted to do something to help other moms who have lost their babies, and so Timothy's Hope was started. I have a personalised care package I put together to send to loss mamas. I hope to eventually be able to send these out free of charge, but am not yet in a position financially to be able to do this. Each package cost is just the cost of the items in them and part of the shipping. I foot all costs of my time and partial shipping costs. I just hope that through the loss of my babies and the care packages I put together we can offer grieving mamas some comfort. We are on Etsy as Timothy's Hope.

My babies have changed me. I will never be the same. We obviously wish things could have gone differently, but we try to find comfort in the fact that they will never have to deal with the troubles and sadness of earth. All they know is peace and eternal joy. We may not understand why Timothy and Morgan had to leave us so soon, but we mortals can only see a small piece of the eternal picture. God sees the whole picture, and someday we will understand His plan.

It wasn't supposed to be this way. You were supposed to grow up and live and laugh and love.

It wasn't supposed to be this way. I was supposed to carry you for 9 months before bringing you into this world.

It wasn't supposed to be this way. Because of COVID your daddy couldn't be there when I found out you were gone.

It wasn't supposed to be this way. Babies aren't supposed to die.

And God said, *'No, it wasn't supposed to be this way. But behold, I am making all things new.'*

lost & found

by Jacqueline Waters

I didn't mean to have an abortion. I simply didn't know I was pregnant.

There I was all prepped for tubal ligation and the nurse said to me, 'We know you don't want to be pregnant, so we do a D & C just in case you are.'

It hadn't occurred to me I might be pregnant, and I hadn't known in advance about the D & C, so I hadn't given the matter any thought. I shrugged off any doubts and abandoned myself to the procedure. My husband and I had our pigeon pair, and as we settled into our new lives in Australia, there were challenges enough without becoming pregnant. Back then I wasn't walking with Jesus, who would have provided friends, wisdom, and grace.

Many years later I invited Jesus to step into my life and turn it around. Then began a journey of allowing Him to clean up all the wounds I had suffered through my own wrong choices. Step by step He brought me to wholeness in my soul, with divine wisdom choosing the right moment to recall the situations that had damaged me, and powerfully reversing the effects of wrong decisions I had made.

One day, through circumstances only God could have arranged, I found myself talking with a prayer counsellor who was a fellow guest at a friend's home. My friend had gone out for the day, and Janet and I were getting to know one another, sharing ideas and personal stories. Suddenly her expression became more focussed and serious.

'I'm discerning a spirit of death on your uterus,' she said simply, but gently.

I hadn't thought about my uterus much since I'd given up the need for it, and in any case, I'd been divorced for years.

'Have you ever had an abortion or a miscarriage?' she asked, trying to help me find a reason for what she was discerning.

'No', I said, sure of my facts. But then genius Holy Spirit went to work and vivid memories of that pre-op conversation with the nurse flooded my mind. Could it really be true that I had unwittingly killed my unborn child? Even though I had not wanted another pregnancy, I knew I never would have deliberately disposed of a human life, no matter how small. But under the pure light of the Holy Spirit's illumination, the awful truth dawned on me. A flood of negative emotions engulfed me: horror and guilt for my part in allowing it, grief for my loss, sorrow for my child, and regret that I had not known her.

Gently Holy Spirit set to work in my heart as Janet led me through a prayerful process of dealing with those emotions. Firstly, I asked for forgiveness. It was a sin committed in ignorance, but a sin, nevertheless. The blood of the Saviour was more than enough to cleanse it away, and the weight of guilt and self-recrimination lifted off. Then I had to hand over my regrets to the Lord. Regret wasn't going to undo anything. Janet prayed for my womb to be delivered from the spirit of death that had taken advantage of my ignorance so many years previously. The spiritual side of my problem was dealt with. My soul was still in pain.

But Holy Spirit wasn't finished. The Lord revealed the sex of the child – a girl. She was more than a ten-day old foetus; she was a living person. I named her Amanda and surrendered her to her heavenly Father. She was already with him, of course, but now I knew about her, I needed to release her from my heart to the loving care of Heaven. Then healing began in my soul. It went on for quite a while, as I came to terms with this new knowledge. I shed tears on her behalf, that she'd been snatched away so soon after her conception. I shed tears for my own grief – that my arms had never held her tiny form, that I'd never played with her, never taught her to speak or to read. I didn't know what her gifts were – would she have been an athlete, a singer, or a writer? I didn't know her favourite colour, or if she liked Vegemite. But God had more to reveal.

One day I was reading in *Heaven is for Real* by Todd Burpo, a little boy's account of a heavenly visitation where he met his sister, who had been miscarried. I thought about Amanda, growing up in heaven. Almost audibly I heard the Lord say,

'You will see Amanda in heaven, and she will call you "Mum".' I wept, undone by His love and His grace. The reality of her existence, of her eternal relationship with me, impacted me afresh. We would have eternity to get to know one another, to enjoy adventures together. When our all-powerful God says He restores all things, He means it.

On another occasion, I was worshipping with friends, when I was transported briefly into heavenly realms and saw Amanda. She had brown curly hair and blue eyes that sparkled with radiant happiness. I have been told that children grow up more slowly in heaven and she looked about eight years old, not the adult she would have been in earth years. I wonder how old she will be when I join her. I am so grateful that through God's grace I can look forward to meeting her one day and to spending eternity with her. Meanwhile my heart is at rest, and so is hers.

the meteorite

by Ayla Grace

My pregnancy was unexpected, and the loss of my pregnancy even more so. I felt that within a matter of days my life had been completely upended. I struggled for a long time to put words to what it felt like. After one particularly heart-wrenching weekend of grief, I realised what it felt like. It felt like a meteorite.
This is the writing from that weekend.

Part 1

My garden was good. Not perfect. Not without scars, but good enough. I had patched up areas that needed patching up, I had tended to all the minor bumps I had had along the way. But what I most remember is that I was happy. Content. It felt that my life, my garden, was as it should be.

As I was standing in my garden on an ordinary evening... Admiring the sky, thinking of the different and new options I might take in my garden... What I was dreaming of to plant and change... I noticed that the clouds began growing dark.

And I heard a whizzing sound in the air. Was it a plane? It was odd for it to be so close to my garden. I couldn't put my finger on what exactly it was. But it was getting louder. And closer.

At first I was nervous. And then I was excited. There was a special arrival coming! I hadn't invited anyone. God had a surprise for me! For me? I felt so very special and chosen. I was excited to welcome this visitor and grateful to God for bringing an unexpected blessing into my garden, my life.

I had barely finished my prayers of thanksgiving when I caught my breath from the excitement… I bought a pregnancy magazine. I had started remembering the visions God had given me of a daughter. I had explained to several close family and friends just how blessed I felt. I had felt my heart grow to double its size, each new symptom reminding me of how chosen I felt. God's miracles were landing right in my lap for a change! And then… it hit. Utter devastation. This wasn't a visitor.

I don't remember taking the hit. I just remember waking up flat, face down on the now dusty, red earth. With a ringing noise in my ears. A piercing ringing. I looked up and I couldn't see properly. My glasses had been thrown off in the hit. Everything was blurry and desolate. How was I now in a red, dusty desert? And where was my garden? All my plants? My special visitor I was preparing for? Everything I had tended to so carefully for 33 years? Nothing looked like it had before.

I stumbled to my feet, dizzy and disoriented. I was covered in red dirt. I could taste blood in my mouth. I felt blood dripping somewhere down my legs. It was hot. So hot. Was I sweating? My clothes had been ripped open as I flew to the ground. I knew I was injured but I was so cut off from reality, I couldn't figure out exactly how badly injured I was.

Or which body part had been most affected. I was too scared to feel around for anything that might be missing. Was I in a computer game? Had I been transported to Mars? Had the second coming of Jesus happened? And again, where was my garden??? I began to panic.

As I managed to regain balance, I quickly felt around and managed to locate my glasses. Placing them over painful, small cuts on my face took some time, but I had to get a grip on what was going on! I took a long, hard look at what was in front of me. I felt the sting of tears forming in the corners of my eyes. Nothing. It was all gone. What was in front of me was devastating. I couldn't tear myself away from staring at the horror facing me. My baby was dead. No sign of life on the sonar screen.

My body was starting to heave in pain. I only know this because I could see it - I still wasn't feeling it. I looked around and I saw people rushing to me. I saw my husband desperately calling to me. But all I felt was, nothing? I was numb.

My garden was gone. My life forever changed. Where my garden once was, the earth had been violently cracked open. Boulders had been thrown out the earth like tiny flecks of sand in the wind. Steam was rising from the hole caused by this loss. The hole in my life was so big I was again convinced that I surely wasn't on earth any longer. The ringing in my ears wasn't stopping.

I took a few steps closer to the massive hole in front of me. Ignoring the calls and emergency personnel trying to get to me. They'd get to me eventually I remember thinking. I had more important things to do other than physically surviving, right now! I needed to make sense of this hole. And why on earth was I covered in blood and bruises?

I peered cautiously over the edge. What had caused this? The hole was kilometers deep. I peered into the abyss that was unending. I noticed, oddly, that there were a few plants still standing at the very edge of this huge hole - rebellious in their defiance to be taken out by what had arrived without invite. I didn't invite this loss. And I don't believe in a God that would have either. Nothing made sense anymore. I'd come back for these defiant plants one day I remember thinking. And then I saw it at the bottom of this happening hole. My garden had been hit.

By a meteorite. The meteorite of pregnancy loss. The meteorite that I never thought would land in my story, in my garden.

It is a flaming ball, whose only intention is utter devastation. It had uninvited, entered the orbit of my life and obliterated the garden of my life. It never had any intention other than destruction and pain. It was never going to arrive gently... Carefully... Or with an invite. It was always meant to arrive violently and come close to killing me.

Nothing looked the same anymore. I didn't know where to start or what to do. I collapsed in a heap and waited for my husband and emergency personnel to reach me. I couldn't walk. I couldn't think. I couldn't comprehend how my life had been obliterated. I lay there until they got to me. Hoping, praying that maybe this was a terrible dream. Jesus surely didn't choose this path for me.

Part 2

I've since returned to this place. The place of my garden. The place where I almost died. Several times. Each time is no less painful. I've admired the defiant flowers from a distance when I've visited. I'll get to them when I'm stronger. I'll thank them for the hope they've planted in my heart. But right now, the hole is still too big for me to be grateful or thankful for. At least, not as often as I'd like.

On my most recent visit, I saw Jesus sitting on the edge of the hole. His feet dangling. A gentle smile on His face. 'My darling, devastation can be beautiful too. But I know it's too painful to accept that right now. I promise in time, you will. I don't expect you to sit at this hole. You don't need to visit it often. I don't expect you to come back and garden here. Or repair a single thing. That's my job.'

I looked at Him. Grateful for His patience and kindness. And broken at His generosity to repair my garden so miraculously - because it really should take armies of men. I'm still too injured to really appreciate His words. I still have the taste of blood in my mouth. My cuts are still raw. I'm still walking with a painful limp. No one can physically see these wounds. But I feel them in my body and deep in my heart, with every single step. As He sees the pain in my eyes, He leaves the hole and walks to me.

I remember - this is my God. The God that doesn't need me to come to Him.

I feel His arms embrace me. I collapse into His strength. I cry out in pain. I can't tell any longer if it's emotional or physical. It just all hurts. Everything. As I'm trembling, entirely held up by Him... He caresses the top of my head, gently touching a small facial cut that's still raw. He sees it all, every single wound caused. He reminds me: 'My darling, chosen daughter. You don't need to be here. You don't need to relive this. You don't need to be strong. I am repairing this garden. Will you be able to leave it alone? Will you be able to trust I'm replacing this hole with something better than you could have ever imagined?'

My honest answer is no. How do I live my life while this hole still exists? How do I keep going when my garden is gone? How long is this going to take? How long will I need to live like this before the repairs are done? Can't I do something now??? But I look into the eyes of my gentle savior, who is wholly incapable of lying to me and I manage to whisper out a faint 'yes'. I see tears form in His eyes. Is His heart breaking too? Is He also full of grief for the devastating loss I'm having to witness? Surely the King of Kings, who sees the ending of restoration doesn't cry in the pain?

Without me saying a word, He knows my thoughts and feels my pain, deeply. His eyes welled up with tears too and He speaks again. 'Yes. My heart is broken for you my daughter. I know the ending, but right now I am with you in this pain. It was never meant to be this way. I will make sure that your pain is not in vain. I will make sure that what has been lost will be replaced with the most magnificent gifts. This is a promise you can build your life on. Leave this hole with me.'

Part 3

I now have a new, makeshift garden. I need somewhere to exist while God repairs my hole. It's not my old garden. It's different. I didn't choose it. It's been created out of necessity. There's not much in it and it's taking a lot of work to make it even a tenth of what I had. I don't particularly love it. And I definitely don't particularly love the pity as others pass by, offering their condolences. It doesn't make gardening in my new garden any easier.

Sometimes I get angry. Really angry. So angry I feel hotter than the sun bearing down on me. I dig harder. As if that will speed time up. And then the anger wells up in tears and utter, exasperated frustration. I had a garden. I don't want a new one! But I am trying. I'm trying my best to appreciate the new shoots in my new garden. I'm trying my best to be thankful for the new plants God has so generously given to me in this new place. It's not what I tended to for 33 years, but it's what I have now.

While I garden and wait, I often remember my old garden. I keep seeing the big gaping hole in that garden. Trauma does that. Intrusive thoughts you don't want and you definitely didn't invite. This triggers me every single time. I desperately fight the overwhelming urge to take this repair job back from God. To run back and fix it. To fill one million buckets of sand until it's done. Even if I never sleep again. I desperately want this to be in my control. But it's not. Because I can't. Emotionally and physically I can't. It's too big. Too scary. Absolutely impossible for anyone or any multitude of armies to do, but God. He's quick to remind me of that. And to breathe. I hear his still small voice, 'It's just a trauma trigger my darling. Not the truth. Trust me.'

So - I've got this garden to focus on. Not that garden. Not those repairs. I can't do that in my own strength. Sometimes I need to remind myself of this every day. And on tough days, every hour. I often pray in my quiet time for God to help me with this; to recoup my mental health. I've lived through several immense traumas to know that my mind can be my worst enemy in trauma recovery.

So how do I do this? How do I garden in this strange place when I know my other garden exists, but it is full of massive holes and I can't go back? God has asked me, specifically, to leave it to Him.

I remind myself of the promise. I declare it. Over and over and over and over and over and over again. As many times as it takes. I have a promise *because* of the hole. I wouldn't have this promise if the hole wasn't there. God has told me, I can build my life on this. He is going to give me back more than what I've lost. But there's a responsibility on me too. As I garden in this new, strange territory - I must remember this. I must hold up my end of the deal too. I must be faithful in my belief. I must absolutely, 100% for sure, leave the hole to Him. Focusing on what's in front of me, only.

Because friends, here's the hope of all hope. One day He'll call us back. One day He'll show us what He's replaced the hole with. One day you, Him, and me will all dance together on the beautiful, fresh dirt He's used to repair our gardens.

And I can tell you for certain that I will stamp and shout and jump and scream with joy. I'll look around and beam. I will look around and be overwhelmed by the healing. I'll see the incredibly beautiful gifts He's replaced my garden with. The dirt will rise up in clouds of colourful red, brown, yellow, golden dust - in massive celebration. I'll finally release the pain of this chapter and move into my new place in the sun. The sun will feel exhilarating and not painful on this day.

Where I'm at, where we are at, is not forever. It's for now. We are under the protection of the God whose love and faithfulness to us is more than we could ever imagine, with clear orders - while He repairs what has been stolen. Hold onto this promise with all your life.

Hope.

embracing everest

by Stephanie Richmond

Our Baby Everest went to be with Jesus...
Everyone experiences loss and grief so differently. One second your loved one is with you, and then, they are not.

Everyone hears about their own loss differently as well. For us, it was, 'there is no heartbeat.' I'll never forget those words or the moment we heard them or the heart-felt, sympathetic tone that accompanied them.

> There
> is
> no
> heartbeat.

More than that, I'll never forget all that baby Everest has taught me so far – about myself, about others, about life, and about my faith in Christ.

I'm still learning so much. How amazing it is, though, that my unborn child could teach me as much as I've learned!

There's an interesting dance happening with deep, deep sorrow and this peace I feel. One second I can't breathe because the loss feels so heavily painful, and the next, I'm thinking about butter on my pancakes.

I never liked butter on my pancakes until I was pregnant with Everest. And now, that's the only way I can eat them. My heart tugs at the sight of so many things, not just butter.

There are remnants of Everest everywhere – especially at home. But, as I sat at the kitchen table the other morning trying to process the emotions of it all, I was trying to answer. . .

'My baby is special to me because_____.'

I just kept thinking about how much love I have for this baby and all the things I wanted to teach Everest.

And then my heart was flooded with how much more Jesus loves this child. Baby Everest is with the mighty Teacher – the One who loves him/her best. That kind of love is so powerful!

This doesn't take the pain away, but it gives me hope.

Everest will never know pain or suffering of any kind. There's a unique kind of beauty in that.

It's a very surreal place to be – deep in the depths of the valley of grief while being covered with the kind of peace that surpasses all understanding.

So, where do we go from here?

One of the best pieces of wisdom we have received comes from others who have walked before us. . .

'Keep talking about it with each other and with trusted friends and family.'

Something very healing happens when people hold space for you to share your raw, unfiltered emotions.

From the bottom of our hearts, thank you! Thank you to the friends and family who have been holding space for us at all hours of the day and night! Thank you for helping us embrace Everest all the more. Thank you for your unwavering love and prayers!

But they who wait for the Lord shall renew their strength...
Isaiah 40:31

mother of wilde

by Moria Rooney

On March 9, 2021, our second son Noah Wilde's heart stopped unexpectedly when he was 35 weeks old. 'How is this God's plan for us?' This was my first sentence after I heard the words, 'I'm sorry there is no heartbeat.' This journey hasn't been easy but we keep going because for a Christ-follower, nothing is random. Pain has a purpose. In the weeks and months after Noah went to be with Jesus, my husband and I learned to embrace God's presence more than answers. Should unanswered questions and pain change our view of God? He is merciful, powerful, righteous, holy, and just - but when life is tough, do we still describe God in the same ways? We've learned through Noah's life that our suffering and longing for having him physically here does have significance. We've learned that how you heal is up to you. Noah has helped refine our faith in God because we have known what it's like to experience affliction and still be faithful. We have known Him through suffering. And praise the Lord that although we grieve, we grieve with hope in the eternal life that is to come.

father of wilde

by Brian Rooney

Have you ever had your life flipped upside down? What do you do when you go from expecting another baby boy to receiving the news within 24 hours of delivery that, 'your baby has no heartbeat'? So many thoughts enter your mind, and you are overwhelmed with a feeling of numbness. A big question mark is immediately put over your life and you shut down.

You question and blame everything at that moment, including God. I remember feeling so lost, so weak, that I was no longer in control of the outcome. Something we must learn is we are never in control of our outcomes, but we are in control of how we overcome and handle those difficult times, and who we become from them.

When things go bad in our lives, we tend to put blame on God. We must realise that there is also an evil force at work in our life every day and the life we are living on Earth is only temporary. One day I will see my son Noah again. That's the hope I hold onto every single day. The Bible says that the enemy comes to steal, kill, and destroy. He wants your life but most importantly, your mind. After hours, days, months of talking with God and asking Him 'why?', I realised that I may never receive that answer. But I must know and have faith that He is protecting us, someway, somehow.

My faith in Christ has gotten me through some tough times in the past so I know I needed to lean into Him even more, more than I ever have before. A person without faith will have a hard time getting through a situation like this because you will be overcome with negative emotions that will then trickle into your mindset, your relationships, your marriage, and you being a good father to the kids you have already or the ones to come. You can't let it negatively change who you already are. Your life is not about you, it's about Christ living through you.

Having our first-born son, Roman, a year prior was my driving force to not let the enemy take control of my mind. After Noah, I would constantly hear a little voice in my head from the enemy saying, 'God let this happen to Noah 'or 'remember this time or that time', and it would make me so angry inside. I found myself bottling those emotions up and just responding with, 'I'm good' when people asked how I was doing. Then I would hear God's voice on my heart saying to 'let it out, express yourself', which I believe that opening up was the healing aspect that helped me most and still does. Having an amazing wife kept me motivated to want to grow and come out on the other end victorious. And yet I know that God allowed this to happen, I also know that He put His one and only son upon the cross, for us! So, I can easily say that He is ultimately protecting us and wants what is best for our lives here on earth.

Many people don't realise that this is not a decision you make and then everything is okay. No, no, no. This is an everyday choice and battle you struggle with daily - whether it's child loss or past situations where you felt abandoned and left by God.

The teacher is sometimes silent during the tests. Remember, the enemy wants your mind, and it's why he asked Adam and Eve in the garden, 'did God really say that?' He will forcefully try and steer you away from your faith in Christ, he is the master manipulator, and you must always be on guard.

I have, also, come to realise that most of your family and friends won't ask you about your child loss experience or the emotions you have from it. Not many people know what to say or how to say it, so they end up not saying anything at all. If you want your child's legacy and story to live on, then it must be through you.

I am in awe of the mothers that go through child loss. You all are incredible. Watching how my wife handled everything and how she immediately responded in the waiting room after the news struck us with, 'we can't lose our faith', is something I can't wrap my head around. It makes me cry every time I think about it because there's so much passion from that one moment. It's a memory you never want to have but soon it will become your motivating factor.

My wife and I have recently started a company, called Mother of Wilde (Motherofwilde.com), in memory of our son Noah. Our company creates photo prints and gifts for bereaved parents. We specialise in creating child loss prints and, recently, child loss apparel. My wife has been able to form so many genuine relationships with moms and has been able to minister to them. When you think of a calling on your life you never picture it coming from such a tragic experience, but I can easily say that we are walking out our calling.

Losing Noah has inspired me to not make excuses and to go after what God has prepared for me. There's not much support for dads in general and in the child loss community, that support gets even smaller. I pray God will use me to be a light for other fathers that have gone through child loss and help strengthen their faith in Christ. I think it's hard for men to open up and discuss emotions because we are taught to be the leader of our households. So instead, we bottle things up and keep to ourselves like everything is okay when it really isn't. It is healing and healthy when you open up and discuss what's on your heart - you will come to know that.

I thank God every day for the time we had with Noah. I am grateful for God continuing to press into me and even when I don't feel strong enough, He still pursues me. We are blessed for the opportunity to create a legacy that honours Noah and shares his story and our testimony of God's faithfulness for years to come.

Until we see each other again little buddy. Mommy and Daddy love you!

not the end

FROM THE MOMENT I KNEW Shiloh's name, she has been celebrated. Now, she lives – as her name prophesied – in the dwelling place of God.

But that doesn't mean I'm going to stop celebrating her.

Keeping her alive in my memory, as she is alive in the spiritual realm of eternity, is a means of this mother remaining healthy. When I start to forget eternity, when I become lost in the daily grind and remember all the earthly memories I never got to make with my daughter, that's when I slip and tumble into that dark place again. And that's okay. Because in this grief, all feelings are allowed. All feelings can be taken to the throne room of God. He's listening to every cry, catching every tear, and instilling every hope.

He knew even before time began that we would meet on these pages. He knew that when I was a baby myself, I would go to a family's home where they would lose their daughter that night, and that years later He would use that mother's experience to comfort me. To comfort you. For us to know there is restoration to be had in brokenness.

He knew when He gave me Shiloh's name that I would not feel her kick, I would not even see her arms and legs on the ultrasound screen. But He also knew that those strong limbs would come with her perfect body in Heaven.

He knew long before that I would have to write this book for my hope to rise, when I started to see His fingerprints on every page and how He has worked all things together.

He knew that Shiloh Grace Chapman was never intended for this world but He gave me a daughter anyway. He gave me a promise in her name and said, 'Guess what, when you come home, I have so much in store for you!'

He knew I would struggle and cry. He knew I would go to a counsellor's office, dragging my heavy load. He knew I would bleed onto the pages of this book. And He knew, that my story would one day rest in your hands.

Dear one, please know, He knows your journey too. And He loves you. So completely.

This is not the end. It's only the beginning. And if I don't have the pleasure of meeting you earthside, I look forward to seeing you and your precious ones in Heaven.

I'll be the Mama completely wonderstruck. After all, my daughter was so precious that she *had* to exist. And she had to exist solely in the perfect dwelling place of God.

'See, I will create
new heavens and a new earth.
The former things will not be remembered,
nor will they come to mind.
But be glad and rejoice forever
in what I will create,
for I will create Jerusalem to be a delight
and its people a joy.
I will rejoice over Jerusalem
and take delight in my people;
the sound of weeping and of crying
will be heard in it no more.
**Never again will there be in it
an infant who lives but a few days,**
or an old man who does not live out his years;
the one who dies at a hundred
will be thought a mere child;
the one who fails to reach a hundred
will be considered accursed.
They will build houses and dwell in them;
they will plant vineyards and eat their fruit.
No longer will they build houses and others live in them,
or plant and others eat.
For as the days of a tree,
so will be the days of my people;
my chosen ones will long enjoy
the work of their hands.
**They will not labour in vain,
nor will they bear children doomed to misfortune;
for they will be a people blessed by the Lord,**
they and their descendants with them.

Before they call I will answer;
while they are still speaking I will hear.
The wolf and the lamb will feed together,
and the lion will eat straw like the ox,
and dust will be the serpent's food.
They will neither harm nor destroy
on all my holy mountain,'
says the Lord.

ISAIAH 65:17-25

your story

honouring

Amanda
Ayla Grace
Everest
Hannah
Micah
Morgan
Noah Wilde
Raiya Elizabeth
Shiloh Grace
Timothy

forever loved

www.ingramcontent.com/pod-product-compliance
Lightning Source LLC
Chambersburg PA
CBHW070256010526
44107CB00056B/2480